1

2014

Top NAICS Codes
A Guide for Small, Minority-owned and Women-owned Businesses

2

Table of Contents

INTRODUCTION

Our Commitment

The U.S. Department of the Treasury (Treasury) is committed to providing small, minority-owned and women-owned businesses with contracting opportunities to provide products and services throughout the agency as either prime contractors or subcontractors. Commitment to business diversity starts with its top leadership, as articulated by the Treasury Secretary. It is included in the strategic plan of the Department and progress is monitored by senior management on a regular basis. Additionally, attainment of small business goals is part of the performance objectives of all procurement officials.

Treasury procures a broad array of good and services -- ranging from metals, inks and paper for the manufacture of coins and currency to information technology, office supplies and janitorial services to support the daily work of its employees. In recent years, Treasury has spent approximately $7 billion annually in contracts. More than one-third of small business eligible dollars have been awarded to small, minority-owned, and women-owned businesses.
What Treasury Buys

The North American Industry Classification System (NAICS) classifies business establishments for the purpose of collecting, analyzing, and publishing statistical data related to the U.S. economy. (Refer to: www.census.gov/eos/www/naics/.) The NAICS industry codes define establishments based on the activities in which they are primarily engaged. The first step in doing business with Treasury is to identify the NAICS codes for the products or services that the business provides and determining if they are aligned with that NAICS codes for what Treasury buys. (To identify your NAICS code, refer to http://www.naics.com/search/.)

Top NAICS Codes
A Guide for Small, Minority-owned and Women-owned Businesses

When the federal government intends to purchase products or services, it identifies the NAICS code that describes the principal purpose of that procurement. A business may have numerous capabilities, and the NAICS code for a given procurement opportunity may not be the same as the primary NAICS code of the business. That will not keep a business from bidding or making an offer, as long as the business meets the size standard for the procurement and has the capacity to provide the products or services.

Treasury buys a variety of products and services to fulfill its mission. Each year, Treasury publishes the TOP 25 NAICS lists for Treasury overall, its headquarters, and each bureau. The TOP 25 NAICS list is a resource that businesses can use to quickly determine if Treasury is spending a considerable amount of its resources within their NAICS code(s) and can assist businesses in determining marketing strategies. Businesses that provide products and/or services within these industry codes are encouraged to market their business capabilities to Treasury.
Top NAICS Codes: A Guide for Small, Minority-owned and Women-owned Businesses is designed to assist small, minority, and women-owned business owners in identifying what Treasury buys. It includes list of the top NAICS codes for the U.S. Department of the Treasury overall, as well as for the Treasury Headquarters (Departmental Offices) and individual bureaus. It is intended to serve as a convenient reference tool.

The TOP 25 NAICS lists for Treasury also are published online after the close of the previous fiscal year (after September 30) at: www.treasury.gov/about/organizational-structure/offices/Mgt/Pages/dcfo-osdbu-mp-top25.aspx.)

U.S. Department of the Treasury
(Headquarters and Bureaus Combined)

The U.S. Department of the Treasury (Treasury) is the steward of the U.S. economy – taking in revenue, paying bills, and, when appropriate, borrowing and investing public funds. In more recent years, Treasury's role has expanded to being a leader in safeguarding and growing the nation's economy. Treasury is organized into the headquarters (Departmental Offices), operating bureaus, and inspectors general.

Total FY13 Small Business Eligible Dollars Obligated: $2,111,926,216
Total FY13 Small Business Dollars Obligated: $826,902,836

Website: www.treasury.gov

Address: U.S. Department of the Treasury
1500 Pennsylvania Ave. NW
Washington, DC 20220

Top NAICS Codes
A Guide for Small, Minority-owned and Women-owned Businesses

List of Major NAICS Codes

541519	Other Computer Related Services
541512	Computer Systems Design Services
322121	Paper (Except Newsprint) Mills
517110	Wired Telecommunications Carriers
511210	Software Publishers
334111	Electronic Computer Manufacturing
541611	Administrative Management and General Management Consulting Services
541511	Custom Computer Programming Services
443120	Computer and Software Stores
325910	Printing Ink Manufacturing
561499	All Other Business Support Services
493110	General Warehousing and Storage
561210	Facilities Support Services
541513	Computer Facilities Management Services
541618	Other Management Consulting Services
541990	All Other Professional, Scientific, And Technical Services
221122	Electric Power Distribution
561612	Security Guards and Patrol Services
561720	Janitorial Services
323111	Commercial Printing (Except Screen and Books)
532420	Office Machinery and Equipment Rental and Leasing
518210	Data Processing, Hosting, And Related Services
541211	Offices of Certified Public Accountants
611420	Computer Training
561621	Security Systems Services (Except Locksmiths)

Treasury Headquarters
(Departmental Offices)

The Departmental Offices are primarily responsible for policy formulation and overall management of Treasury. The bureaus are primarily the operating units of the organization.

Total FY13 Small Business Eligible Dollars Obligated: **$251,782,572**
Total FY13 Small Business Dollars Obligated: **$115,809,970**

Website: www.treasury.gov

Small Business Contact: **LaTonya D. Richardson**
Phone: (240) 613-8600
Address: c/o Internal Revenue Service
6009 Oxon Hill Rd
Constellation Centre - 7th Floor
Oxon Hill, MD 20745
Email: AWSS.SBRO@treasury.gov

List of Major NAICS Codes

493110	General Warehousing and Storage
541611	Administrative Management and General Management Consulting Services
928120	International Affairs
541511	Custom Computer Programming Services
541110	Offices of Lawyers
541990	All Other Professional, Scientific, and Technical Services
561110	Office Administrative Services
541614	Process, Physical Distribution, and Logistics Consulting Services
541211	Offices of Certified Public Accountants
519190	All Other Information Services
541519	Other Computer Related Services
522310	Mortgage and Nonmortgage Loan Brokers
236220	Commercial and Institutional Building Construction
541513	Computer Facilities Management Services
561410	Document Preparation Services
541720	Research and Development in the Social Sciences and Humanities
517110	Wired Telecommunications Carriers
541820	Public Relations Agencies
518210	Data Processing, Hosting, And Related Services
519130	Internet Publishing and Broadcasting and Web Search Portals
561720	Janitorial Services
541219	Other Accounting Services
541330	Engineering Services
561210	Facilities Support Services
561450	Credit Bureaus

Alcohol and Tobacco Tax and Trade Bureau (TTB)

The Alcohol and Tobacco Tax and Trade Bureau (TTB) is responsible for enforcing and administering laws covering the production, use, and distribution of alcohol and tobacco products. TTB also collects excise taxes for firearms and ammunition.

Total FY13 Small Business Eligible Dollars Obligated: $23,205,837
Total FY13 Small Business Dollars Obligated: $15,126,592

Website: www.ttb.gov

Small Business Contact: **Cheryl Rice-Henderson**
Phone: (202) 453-1038
Address: Alcohol and Tobacco Tax and Trade Bureau
                           1310 G Street, NW, Box 12
                           Washington, DC 20005
Email: SmallBusinessSpec@ttb.gov

Top NAICS Codes
A Guide for Small, Minority-owned and Women-owned Businesses

List of Major NAICS Codes

236220	Commercial and Institutional Building Construction
334111	Electronic Computer Manufacturing
334112	Computer Storage Device Manufacturing
334119	Other Computer Peripheral Equipment Manufacturing
334516	Analytical Laboratory Instrument Manufacturing
334611	Software Reproducing
339944	Carbon Paper and Inked Ribbon Manufacturing
423430	Computer and Computer Peripheral Equipment and Software Merchant Wholesalers
485111	Mixed Mode Transit Systems
485113	Bus and Other Motor Vehicle Transit Systems
511210	Software Publishers
517210	Wireless Telecommunications Carriers (Except Satellite)
518210	Data Processing, Hosting, And Related Services
519130	Internet Publishing and Broadcasting and Web Search Portals
519190	All Other Information Services
532420	Office Machinery and Equipment Rental and Leasing
532490	Other Commercial and Industrial Machinery and Equipment Rental and Leasing
541380	Testing Laboratories
541511	Custom Computer Programming Services
541512	Computer Systems Design Services
541519	Other Computer Related Services
541910	Marketing Research and Public Opinion Polling
561621	Security Systems Services (Except Locksmiths)
611420	Computer Training
811219	Other Electronic and Precision Equipment Repair and Maintenance

Bureau of Engraving & Printing (BEP)

The Bureau of Engraving & Printing (BEP) designs and manufactures U.S. currency, securities, and other official certificates and awards.

Total FY13 Small Business Eligible Dollars Obligated: **$407,435,547**
Total FY13 Small Business Dollars Obligated: **$61,178,290**

Website: www.moneyfactory.gov

Small Business Contact: **Bernadine Stewart**
Phone: (202) 874-3236
Address: Bureau of Engraving & Printing
  14th & C Streets, SW
  Room 705A
  Washington, DC 20228
Email: bernadine.stewart@bep.gov

List of Major NAICS Codes

322121	Paper (Except Newsprint) Mills
325910	Printing Ink Manufacturing
541512	Computer Systems Design Services
323111	Commercial Printing (Except Screen and Books)
333244	Printing Machinery and Equipment Manufacturing
325220	Artificial and Synthetic Fibers and Filaments Manufacturing
541519	Other Computer Related Services
561210	Facilities Support Services
323119	Other Commercial Printing
221122	Electric Power Distribution
561720	Janitorial Services
423840	Industrial Supplies Merchant Wholesalers
423430	Computer and Computer Peripheral Equipment and Software Merchant Wholesalers
221330	Steam and Air-Conditioning Supply
541712	Research and Development in the Physical, Engineering, and Life Sciences (Except Biotechnology)
221119	Other Electric Power Generation
452910	Warehouse Clubs and Supercenters
541511	Custom Computer Programming Services
325998	All Other Miscellaneous Chemical Product and Preparation Manufacturing
562211	Hazardous Waste Treatment and Disposal
423710	Hardware Merchant Wholesalers
517110	Wired Telecommunications Carriers
561990	All Other Support Services
561621	Security Systems Services (Except Locksmiths)
326299	All Other Rubber Product Manufacturing

Bureau of the Fiscal Service

The Bureau of the Fiscal Service was formed from the consolidation of the Financial Management Service and the Bureau of the Public Debt. Its mission is to promote the financial integrity and operational efficiency of the U.S. government through exceptional accounting, financing, collections, payments, and shared services.

Total FY13 Small Business Eligible Dollars Obligated: $91,482,090
Total FY13 Small Business Dollars Obligated: $71,115,900

Website: www.fiscal.treasury.gov

Small Business Contact:	**Kimberly Witcher**
Phone:	(202) 874-5213
Address:	Bureau of the Fiscal Service
	401 14th Street SW, Suite 270C
	Washington, DC 20227
Email:	Kimberly.witcher@fiscal.treasury.gov

Small Business Contact:	**Loretta Osuna-Cotto**
Phone:	(304) 480-8717
Address:	Bureau of the Fiscal Service
	200 3rd Street, Avery 5F
	Parkersburg, WV 26106-1328
Email:	Loretta.Osuna-Cotto@fiscal.treasury.gov

List of Major NAICS Codes

221112	Fossil Fuel Electric Power Generation
334111	Electronic Computer Manufacturing
334112	Computer Storage Device Manufacturing
334113	Computer Terminal Manufacturing
334118	Computer Terminal and Other Computer Peripheral Equipment Manufacturing
334310	Audio and Video Equipment Manufacturing
423430	Computer and Computer Peripheral Equipment and Software Merchant Wholesalers
443120	Computer and Software Stores
481111	Scheduled Passenger Air Transportation
484210	Used Household and Office Goods Moving
511199	All Other Publishers
511210	Software Publishers
517110	Wired Telecommunications Carriers
523999	Miscellaneous Financial Investment Activities
532420	Office Machinery and Equipment Rental and Leasing
541211	Offices of Certified Public Accountants
541219	Other Accounting Services
541511	Custom Computer Programming Services
541512	Computer Systems Design Services
541519	Other Computer Related Services
541611	Administrative Management and General Management Consulting Services
561210	Facilities Support Services
561320	Temporary Help Services
561720	Janitorial Services
611420	Computer Training

Community Development Financial Institution (CDFI) Fund

The Community Development Financial Institution (CDFI) Fund was created to expand the availability of credit, investment capital, and financial services in distressed urban and rural communities.

Total FY13 Small Business Eligible Dollars Obligated: $7,873,811
Total FY13 Small Business Dollars Obligated: $4,049,617

Website: www.cdfifund.gov

Small Business Contact:	**Telma Holmes**
Phone:	(202) 653-0325
Address:	Community Development Financial Institution (CDFI) Fund
	1801 L Street, NW, Room 6223
	Washington, DC 20036
Email:	Holmest@cdfi.treas.gov

Top NAICS Codes
A Guide for Small, Minority-owned and Women-owned Businesses

List of Major NAICS Codes

492110	Couriers and Express Delivery Services
517212	Cellular and Other Wireless Telecommunications
519190	All Other Information Services
523920	Portfolio Management
523930	Investment Advice
532420	Office Machinery and Equipment Rental and Leasing
541219	Other Accounting Services
541511	Custom Computer Programming Services
541512	Computer Systems Design Services
541519	Other Computer Related Services
541611	Administrative Management and General Management Consulting Services
541620	Environmental Consulting Services
541820	Public Relations Agencies
561320	Temporary Help Services
561450	Credit Bureaus
611430	Professional and Management Development Training

Financial Crimes Enforcement Network (FinCEN)

The Financial Crimes Enforcement Network (FinCEN) supports law enforcement investigative efforts and fosters interagency and global cooperation against domestic and international financial crimes. It also provides U.S. policy makers with strategic analyses of domestic and worldwide trends and patterns.

Total FY13 Small Business Eligible Dollars Obligated: $31,088,053
Total FY13 Small Business Dollars Obligated: $16,444,947

Website: www.fincen.gov

Address: Financial Crimes Enforcement Network
             2070 Chain Bridge Road
             Vienna, VA 22027

Top NAICS Codes
A Guide for Small, Minority-owned and Women-owned Businesses

List of Major NAICS Codes

561499	All Other Business Support Services
541519	Other Computer Related Services
541990	All Other Professional, Scientific, and Technical Services
541513	Computer Facilities Management Services
423430	Computer and Computer Peripheral Equipment and Software Merchant Wholesalers
532420	Office Machinery and Equipment Rental and Leasing
443120	Computer and Software Stores
541612	Human Resources Consulting Services, Human Resources and Executive Search Consulting Services
561320	Temporary Help Services
511199	All Other Publishers
518210	Data Processing, Hosting, And Related Services
511120	Periodical Publishers
511140	Directory and Mailing List Publishers
812930	Parking Lots and Garages
561612	Security Guards and Patrol Services
517911	Telecommunications Resellers
423420	Office Equipment Merchant Wholesalers
721110	Hotels (Except Casino Hotels) and Motels
323113	Commercial Screen Printing
541511	Custom Computer Programming Services
517919	All Other Telecommunications
511130	Book Publishers
511210	Software Publishers
541512	Computer Systems Design Services
517410	Satellite Telecommunications

Internal Revenue Service (IRS)

The Internal Revenue Service (IRS) is the largest of Treasury's bureaus. It is responsible for determining, assessing, and collecting internal revenue in the United States.

Total FY13 Small Business Eligible Dollars Obligated: **$1,648,306,663**
Total FY13 Small Business Dollars Obligated: **$581,298,790**

Website: www.irs.gov

Headquarters

Small Business Contact:	**LaTonya D. Richardson**
Phone:	(240) 613-8600
Address:	Internal Revenue Service
	6009 Oxon Hill Rd
	Constellation Centre - 7th Floor
	Oxon Hill, MD 20745
Email:	AWSS.SBRO@treasury.gov

Northeast Area Office

Small Business Contact:	**Peter Dinicola**
Cheryl Richardson (alt.)	
Phone:	(212) 436-1471 or (212) 436-1518
Address:	Internal Revenue Service
	290 Broadway, 3rd Floor
	New York, NY 10007-1867
Email:	Peter.Dinicola@irs.gov
	Cheryl.J.Richardson@irs.gov

Southeast Area Office

Small Business Contact: **Sandra Dubose**
Phone: (404) 338-9221
Address: 2888 Woodcock Blvd.
Suite 300, Stop 80-N
Atlanta, GA 30341
Email: sandra.dubose@irs.gov

Mid-States Area Office

Small Business Contact: **Cheryl Hill**
Al Monsalve (alt.)

Phone: (972) 308-1925 or (972) 308-1987
Address: Internal Revenue Service
4050 Alpha Road
1045-NDAL, 9th Floor
Dallas, TX 75244-4203
Email: Cheryl.E.Hill@irs.gov
Al.Monsalve@irs.gov

Western Area Office

Small Business Contact: **Denise Alvarez**
Phone: (510) 637 2133
Address: Internal Revenue Service
1301 Clay Street, Suite 810S
Oakland, CA 94512
Email: denise.alvarez@irs.gov

List of Major NAICS Codes

541519	Other Computer Related Services
541512	Computer Systems Design Services
517110	Wired Telecommunications Carriers
334111	Electronic Computer Manufacturing
511210	Software Publishers
443120	Computer and Software Stores
541511	Custom Computer Programming Services
541618	Other Management Consulting Services
541611	Administrative Management and General Management Consulting Services
561210	Facilities Support Services
561499	All Other Business Support Services
561612	Security Guards and Patrol Services
541990	All Other Professional, Scientific, And Technical Services
334119	Other Computer Peripheral Equipment Manufacturing
221122	Electric Power Distribution
492110	Couriers and Express Delivery Services
611420	Computer Training
532420	Office Machinery and Equipment Rental and Leasing
561720	Janitorial Services
518210	Data Processing, Hosting, And Related Services
238220	Plumbing, Heating, and Air-Conditioning Contractors
811212	Computer and Office Machine Repair and Maintenance
541219	Other Accounting Services
511120	Periodical Publishers
561611	Investigation Services

Office of the Comptroller of the Currency (OCC)

The Office of the Comptroller of the Currency (OCC) charters, regulates, and supervises all national banks and federal savings associations. It also supervises the federal branches and agencies of foreign banks. Its goal in supervising banks and federal savings associations is to ensure that they operate in a safe and sound manner and in compliance with laws requiring fair treatment of their customers and fair access to credit and financial products.

Total FY13 Small Business Eligible Dollars Obligated: $153,251,606
Total FY13 Small Business Dollars Obligated: $72,916,429

Website: www.occ.treas.gov

Small Business Contact: **Rhonda Trent**
Phone: (202) 649-6621
Address: Office of the Comptroller of the Currency
400 7th Street, SW
Washington, DC 20219
Email. Rhonda.Trent@occ.treas.gov

List of Major NAICS Codes

541519	Other Computer Related Services
541513	Computer Facilities Management Services
531210	Offices of Real Estate Agents and Brokers
541512	Computer Systems Design Services
524210	Insurance Agencies and Brokerages
541611	Administrative Management and General Management Consulting Services
518210	Data Processing, Hosting, And Related Services
334111	Electronic Computer Manufacturing
541690	Other Scientific and Technical Consulting Services
511210	Software Publishers
541511	Custom Computer Programming Services
541614	Process, Physical Distribution, and Logistics Consulting Services
517210	Wireless Telecommunications Carriers (Except Satellite)
443120	Computer and Software Stores
334290	Other Communications Equipment Manufacturing
532420	Office Machinery and Equipment Rental and Leasing
541310	Architectural Services
722320	Caterers
518111	Internet Service Providers
524114	Direct Health and Medical Insurance Carriers
561320	Temporary Help Services
561210	Facilities Support Services
541990	All Other Professional, Scientific, And Technical Services
561510	Travel Agencies
541211	Offices of Certified Public Accountants

Top NAICS Codes
A Guide for Small, Minority-owned and Women-owned Businesses

U.S. Mint

The U.S. Mint designs and manufactures domestic, bullion and foreign coins as well as commemorative medals and other numismatic items. The Mint also distributes U.S. coins to the Federal Reserve banks as well as maintains physical custody and protection of our nation's silver and gold assets.

Website: www.usmint.gov

Total FY13 Small Business Eligible Dollars Obligated: $4,034,561,491
Total FY13 Small Business Dollars Obligated: $3,380,892,550

Small Business Contact:	**Pauletta Rawlings**
Phone:	(202) 354-8334
Address:	U.S. Mint
	801 Ninth Street, NW
	Washington, DC 20220
Email:	Pauletta.Wyatt@usmint.treas.gov

List of Major NAICS Codes

561499	All Other Business Support Services
541512	Computer Systems Design Services
321999	All Other Miscellaneous Wood Product Manufacturing
541519	Other Computer Related Services
531190	Lessors of Other Real Estate Property
561621	Security Systems Services (Except Locksmiths)
423830	Industrial Machinery and Equipment Merchant Wholesalers
236210	Industrial Building Construction
326199	All Other Plastics Product Manufacturing
541511	Custom Computer Programming Services
423430	Computer and Computer Peripheral Equipment and Software Merchant Wholesalers
221330	Steam and Air-Conditioning Supply
326130	Laminated Plastics Plate, Sheet (Except Packaging), and Shape Manufacturing
322221	Coated and Laminated Packaging Paper and Plastics Film Manufacturing
541330	Engineering Services
238220	Plumbing, Heating, and Air-Conditioning Contractors
325211	Plastics Material and Resin Manufacturing
493110	General Warehousing and Storage
541810	Advertising Agencies
541990	All Other Professional, Scientific, And Technical Services
321920	Wood Container and Pallet Manufacturing
323110	Commercial Lithographic Printing
423840	Industrial Supplies Merchant Wholesalers
541910	Marketing Research and Public Opinion Polling
561720	Janitorial Services

Top NAICS Codes
A Guide for Small, Minority-owned and Women-owned Businesses

Finding Forecasts of Treasury Contract Opportunities

Public Law 100-656, the Business Opportunity Development Reform Act of 1988, amended the Small Business Act to emphasize acquisition planning. The law requires agencies to compile and make available projections of contracting opportunities that small businesses may be able to perform, including Historically Underutilized Business Zone (HUBZone) small businesses and Service Disabled Veteran Owned (SDVOB) small businesses. HUBZone and SDVOB small businesses are encouraged to market their capabilities to Treasury to assist us with our various small business acquisition strategies.

The Department of the Treasury Forecast of Contract Opportunities includes projections of anticipated contract actions above $150,000 that small businesses may be able to perform under direct contracts with Treasury, or perform part of the effort through subcontract arrangements with Treasury's large business prime contractors. For additional information on procurements not expected to exceed $150,000, please contact the appropriate Treasury Bureau Small Business Specialist.

We are committed to increasing prime contract awards and subcontract awards to the small business community. By helping firms identify procurement opportunities as early in the acquisition process as possible, we hope to improve communication with industry and assist the small, minority- and women-owned business community with its marketing efforts.

To see the detailed list of the most recent Forecast of Contract Opportunities go to: http://www.treasury.gov/resource-center/sb-programs/Pages/dcfo-osdbu-mp-forecast.aspx

www.ingramcontent.com/pod-product-compliance
Lightning Source LLC
Chambersburg PA
CBHW080627180526
45168CB00007B/3077